Sticker History

VIKINGS
Sticker Book

Licensed exclusively to Top That Publishing Ltd
Tide Mill Way, Woodbridge, Suffolk, IP12 1AP, UK
www.topthatpublishing.com
Copyright © 2015 Tide Mill Media
All rights reserved
0 2 4 6 8 9 7 5 3 1
Printed and bound in China

A Viking village

The Vikings were Scandinavians with big boats, big shields and big beards (just the men for the last one!). They explored, traded and raided their way around Europe and further afield from about 790 AD to 1066 AD. Their bloodthirsty raids in search of new lands, slaves and treasure made them feared everywhere they went.

Vikings preserved fish by smoking or drying.

Create your own Viking village sticker scene!

A Viking blacksmith was an important person, and some blacksmiths travelled from village to village, making and repairing all kinds of weapons and tools. Viking blacksmiths learnt new ways to make steel swords that were both strong and flexible.

Spurs for horse-riding

Belt buckles

Stick some arrowheads here!

Arrowheads

Stick some belt buckles here!

Hang a cooking pot here!

Cooking pan

Lock and key

Is it hot in here, or is it me?

Iron rods were hammered and twisted together to make a sword blade.

A sword needed to be strong enough to cut through a shield, but flexible enough not to snap or break.

Stick some more nails here!

Iron nails for shipbuilding

Fishing

Viking life revolved around the sea, so it's not surprising that Vikings ate a lot of seafood. Fish, sea mammals, oysters, mussels and shrimp were all regularly on the menu. Fishing boats were small and shallow and fishermen used both nets and lines with hooks to catch fish.

A beached whale was a very exciting find! Whale blubber was a valuable resource.

Walrus hides were cut into thin strips then twisted to make rope.

Fish could be preserved by salting in barrels. The barrels were useful on long expeditions.

Hunting for seals and walruses was dangerous. A walrus could easily weigh over 1 tonne!

Fill the net with fish and crabs!

Seabirds and their eggs made tasty snacks ... whoops!

Inside a Viking house

Vikings built their houses out of whatever was available – stone, wood and even turf! At the centre of the single room was a fire, which provided light and also the heat to cook with. Only the rich had chairs or proper beds! The whole Viking family slept, ate and worked in this one room.

Raised platforms around the edge of the room were used for sleeping.

Add a Viking dad here!

Stick a comb here!

Women kept the key to the chest where all the family valuables were kept, and they were in charge if the husband was away.

Vikings were always combing their hair ... it helped get rid of fleas and nits ... ouch!

Many houses had turf roofs – good for keeping the warmth in.
Loom for making clothes
Balance a chicken and a sheep here!
Hang a big pot here!
Stick a pot here!
In the winter, farm animals were often kept indoors; it kept the animals safe, and the room warmer (but smellier!) too.
Meat stews were cooked in a big pot.
A Viking child's life wasn't easy ... a third of Vikings died in childhood.

Viking clothes

Most clothes were made at home. Men wore tunics and trousers, and women wore long dresses. Only rich jarls could afford expensive colours, beautiful embroidery, and imported silk. Scandinavia can get very cold, so a thick wool cloak and a hat were essential in winter!

Use stickers to dress this Viking jarl.

Going shopping

Craftsmen in a Viking town made and sold most things a family needed. If the town was important enough, then Viking or foreign traders might come to sell their goods. Coins weren't very common, and most trading was done by bartering – swapping one thing for another.

Sports and games

Vikings loved sports, and the rougher and tougher the better! Wrestling, fighting, boulder carrying and spear throwing were all popular. Swimming, sailing and mountain climbing were for the summer months, but when the snow and ice of winter arrived, it was time to get out the skis, sledges and ice skates!

I'm a Norse Horse!

I'm a hiking Viking!

Vikings loved horse fighting. It was a violent and gruesome contest.

Board and dice games were both popular.

Ice skate blades were made from shaped bone.

Create your own Sports and games sticker scene!

Ships and shipbuilding

When we think of Vikings, we think of their ships. Vikings were expert shipbuilders and built various types of craft, including cargo ships and smaller rowing boats. However, the most famous and feared were the long, shallow boats built for war and raiding, known as 'dragonships', or 'longships'.

Stick a carved head here!

Planks were held together using iron rivets. Any gaps were sealed with tar-coated moss or hair.

Add a busy Viking here!

Viking ships had a keel to give the boat stability. This made them easier to steer when sailing.

Add a Viking chipping wood here!

Adze for shaping wood

The whale road

Vikings were great sailors and explorers, and they set out from Scandinavia in search of new land and riches. Voyages were dangerous and uncomfortable; the crew were exposed to the weather, and slept on the deck in leather sleeping bags. Ships sailed along the coast if possible, but long trips could mean weeks at sea!

North America

In about AD 1000, Eric the Red's son, Leif the Lucky, landed in North America ... hundreds of years before Christopher Columbus 'discovered' it!

Greenland

Greenland was explored by Eric the Red. He had been forced to leave Iceland, when he was accused of murder.

At least one crew member bailed water constantly.

The North Pole

Add ships, polar bears, whales and buildings to the Viking map.

Iceland

Scandinavia

Russia

Europe

Viking explorers settled in Russia, Germany, England, Scotland, Ireland, Iceland, Greenland and even North America!

Sailors used landmarks, clouds and sealife to judge where they were. The sun and stars showed how far north they were.

Rowing and riddles

If the wind died down, a longship was rowed, instead of sailed. Rowing was also the safest way to take a longship down narrow channels or rivers. Vikings loved riddles, and they were probably a good way to pass the time. These riddles below are real Viking brain-benders.

Ready to fight!

Unlike modern armies, Vikings had to provide their own equipment ... so weapons varied according to what each warrior could afford. A rich chieftain might carry a sword and wear a chain-mail shirt and a metal helmet. A poorer warrior fought with an axe or a spear, and could only afford a leather helmet.

A good sword was handed down from father to son, and was given a name ... like 'leg-biter'!

Leather helmet with metal strips

Stick an iron helmet here!

Battle-axe

Stick a sword here!

Leather tunic

Stick a wooden shield here!

Chain-mail tunic

Stick a knife here!

Sword sheath

Real Viking helmets didn't have horns or wings on them!

Attack!

In 793 AD, Vikings attacked the monastery of Lindisfarne. It was their first planned raid on England, and was an easy target, as monks didn't have weapons. Raids took place again and again over the following decades. When possible, Vikings simply took what they wanted ... but sometimes, the Anglo-Saxon natives put up a fight!

Create your own Attack sticker scene!

Plunder

Monasteries were full of valuables including tools, gold, jewels and precious books. Not that Vikings were keen on reading – if they found a book with golden clasps, they were ripped off and melted to make new jewellery. Perhaps the most valuable plunder of all were the slaves Vikings captured.

Celebration feast

The successful return of a raiding party called for a celebration! The jarl laid on a feast with plenty of food and drink, and invited all his men. There was music, singing, and best of all, a poet called a 'skald' who told famous stories of Viking gods, kings and ancient heroes.

Skol!

Skol!

Add horns here!

Stick a lyre here!

Stories and poems were told from memory, not written down.

Feasts were also held for funerals and festivals. A really good feast could last for days ... hic!

Stick a roasting pig here!

Vikings drank out of hollow horns. You couldn't put them down ... so you had to drink the whole thing!

Add a horn!

Add a horn!

Stick cheese here!

Add some fish here!

Ale was an everyday drink – even children drank it! Mead was made from honey and drunk at celebrations.

After death

A Viking killed in battle hoped to join the god Odin in Valhalla. It was the best place a Viking could imagine – with fighting every day and feasting every night! Some Vikings were buried, others were cremated or buried at sea. The wealthiest chieftains were laid in a ship which was either buried or set alight.

The ship included everything needed in the afterlife – including food, drink, clothes and beautiful treasures.

Create your own After death sticker scene!

The Gods of Asgard

Vikings believed in many different gods and supernatural beings. But, gradually, Viking kings converted to Christianity. By the year 1000 AD, most Viking areas were Christian, and raids on other Christian countries were greatly reduced. By 1066 AD, the Normans had conquered England, and the Viking Age was over.

Add a raven!

Add a raven!

I'm Odin, the ruler of the Viking gods. I lived in Valhalla, a majestic hall in the world of Asgard.

I'm Frigg, Odin's wife. I could see into the future, but I never told anyone what I saw.

I'm Odin's son Thor. I used a hammer as a weapon, and protected the Vikings.

Stick Thor's hammer here!

The words 'Thursday' and 'Friday' come from 'Thor's day' and 'Frigg's day'.

Many Vikings wore a protective amulet in the shape of Thor's hammer.

Gods sometimes battled against giants. The giants weren't always enemies, though. Gods and giants even married each other!

At the blacksmith's

Fishing

Inside a
Viking house

Viking
village sticker
scene

Viking clothes

Going
shopping

The whale road

Sports and games
sticker scene

Ships and
shipbuilding

Ready to fight!

Plunder

Rowing and
riddles

Celebration
feast